SARIS and a SINGLE MALT

Sweta Srivastava Vikram

From the World Voices Series

Modern History Press

Ann Arbor • London • Sydney

Saris and a Single Malt.
Copyright © 2016 by Sweta Srivastava Vikram.
All Rights Reserved.

ISBN 978-1-61599-294-2 paperback
ISBN 978-1-61599-295-9 eBook

Distributed by Ingram (USA/CAN/AU), Bertrams Books (UK/EU)

Published by
Modern History Press
5145 Pontiac Trail
Ann Arbor, MI 48105

www.ModernHistoryPress.com
info@ModernHistoryPress.com

Tollfree 888-761-6268 (USA/CAN)
Fax 734-663-6861

Library of Congress Cataloging-in-Publication Data

Names: Vikram, Sweta Srivastava, 1975- author.
Title: Saris and a single malt / Sweta Srivastava Vikram.
Description: Ann Arbor, MI : Modern History Press, [2016] | Series: World voices series
Identifiers: LCCN 2016011526| ISBN 9781615992942 (softcover : acid-free paper) | ISBN 9781615992959 (epub, PDF, Kindle)
Subjects: LCSH: Mothers--Death--Poetry.
Classification: LCC PS3622.I493 A6 2016 | DDC 818/.6--dc23
LC record available at https://lccn.loc.gov/2016011526

For Mummy—wherever you are, I am sure the place has good whisky and a beautiful collection of saris.

"The reality is that you will grieve forever. You will not 'get over' the loss of a loved one; you will learn to live with it. You will heal and you will rebuild yourself around the loss you have suffered. You will be whole again but you will never be the same. Nor should you be the same nor would you want to."

~ Elisabeth Kübler-Ross

Contents

Foreword	i
Acknowledgments	ii
FLIGHT	1
Friday, May 30, 2014	2
Destination	3
JFK: Terminal 4 Airport Lounge	4
Wait for Me	5
Looking for Signs	6
Fifty Minutes from New Delhi	7
Serendipity	8
Indira Gandhi International Airport: New Delhi	9
FIRE	10
May 31, 2014	11
Why Didn't You Wait for Me?	12
Crashing	14
It's Not Easy	15
Noise	16
Conversations with Mumma	17
SARIS and a SINGLE MALT	20
Ode to Mumma	21
GRIEF	22
June 1, 2014	23
Does Grief Wear a Color?	24
I Write	25
Forever Courage, Beta	26
Namaste	27
Time Changes Us	28
The Final Note	29
Afterword	30
About the Author	32

Foreword

There are few books like *Saris and a Single Malt* in which the loss of a mother, a homeland, and the self come together in a sustained elegy. Traveling the arc of grief, Sweta Vikram's collection begins with tragic news and continues from there, in real time, as she brings us along on her journey to India to her mother's cremation. Many poems about loss are written after an endured silence, when words just won't come, but in *Saris and a Single Malt*, Vikram sits us next to her on the long flight 'home,' and we hear her cry. We are with her as she is breaking. And we break. It is a privileged and painful journey. Raw and powerful.

Throughout, Vikram is courageous in allowing us to share the nakedness of her grief, the anger, and deception; even the surprise of laughter and joy. And having been privy to this, we feel better equipped to deal with our own grief. *Saris and a Single Malt* shows us how we survive. We are changed by grief. It isn't acceptance one finds, but something in us, which continues to burn on.

—Justen Ahren, Director Noepe Center,
Author of *A Strange Catechism*

Acknowledgments

I wish no one ever had to write a book like *Saris and a Single Malt*—a book about loss and longing and saying goodbye to my mother. I wish no one the pain that provoked the poems and essays in this book.

Having said that, words have a mind of their own. I am grateful that these words presented themselves to me, and that I was able to fashion them into a book that honors my mom. I know she would be pleased.

So many people have helped me through this crisis and made this book possible. I would like to express my gratitude to my cousins in New Delhi, Nishant Sinha and Sushant Sinha, and their respective wives, Tripti Sinha and Mansi Sinha, for opening their homes and hearts. You amaze me. I am humbled by your generosity.

To my relatives and friends in India who reminded me how much love and support surrounds me despite my huge loss, you make me a better person. To those who hurt my feelings, thank you. You, also, have made me stronger, more compassionate, and more determined.

My friends in India, Jaya Sharan and Pooja Gupta Jain, thank you for showing up without me asking, and knowing what I needed. Much gratitude to my friends in New York, especially Leah Zibulsky, Shuchi Sethi, Vivek Yadav, Kerry Bajaj, Karan Bajaj, and Keith Lazarus for not giving up on me when I was at my worst, and for reminding me how blessed I am to have such solid relationships. Special thanks to Sara Goudarzi and Samanta Batra Mehta.

My friend Neetal Adkar in Houston and her mother, dearest Aunty, are the biggest reason why the broken pieces of my heart started to heal. Because of you, my anger turned to forgiveness and my healing began. I owe you so much.

I'd also like to acknowledge Anora McGaha *(When Women Waken)*, Barbara Bos *(Women Writers)*, and Cindy Hochman and Karen Neuberg *(First Literary Review-East) for* giving my poems and essays a home in their journals. To the editorial team at *DoYouYoga*: much gratitude for allowing me to tell my story, "How Not To Be An Obstacle To Your Own Happiness," in a voice that's most authentic to me. Cindy, I so appreciate what you do with your magical proofreading pen.

Papa (my father), Shantanu (*Bhaiya*/older brother), Jyothi (sister-in-law), Diya and Sana (nieces), I remember sharing the raw poems from this book with all of you after Mummy's last rites. We cried together. We laughed together. We worked together to keep her memory alive. I am blessed to have you as my family. You make me a better person and poet.

Grateful thanks to my husband, Anudit, for being my biggest strength and for your encouragement and support as I underwent change and healing in my post-Mom world. My stories exist because of your unconditional faith in me.

My immense gratitude to my literary editor, Sherry Quan Lee, for her astuteness and vision. Doug West, thank you for designing a book cover that is so wonderfully representative of what the book is about. And finally, thank you, Victor R. Volkman, publisher at Modern History Press, for continuing to believe in me.

FLIGHT

Friday, May 30, 2014, my husband and I caught a flight to New Delhi. Mumma, unexpectedly fell ill, and was rushed to the ICU, at Medanta Hospital in Gurgaon. She and my dad were supposed to be on their way to Kashmir—paradise on earth, she said.

Poetry kept me afloat in the air, and after our plane landed. From the time we got the call in New York to the time Mom received last rites 36 hours had passed. In 36 hours the poems in this chapbook took flight.

Friday, May 30, 2014

Poetry, pain, and prayers

I think it is a bad joke—Mumma isn't sick
I had spoken with her two days ago
and promised to cook, *Kalam Polow*
when I saw her next.
She and Papa were headed to Kashmir;
did destiny take a detour?

Mom is put on a ventilator; my thoughts start to breathe.
Her heart is under attack, I feel vulnerable.

I pack my bags,
clean the house,
manage the food in the refrigerator,
reschedule my meetings,
inform a few friends and family
about my sudden trip to India.

My husband, Anudit, smiles and says
you are so much like your Mom.
you even get your meticulousness from her.

Friday, May 30,
I was scheduled to share my poetry at KGB Bar.
I had planned to read poems about my Mom
since it was the month of Mother's Day.
Funny and cheeky poems about how we all become our mothers.

But instead of reading in the East Village,
my husband and I catch a flight to New Delhi.

Poetry never once leaves my hand;
pain and prayers never once leave my pen.

Destination

Do I see myself clearly—
I wonder?
I look for signs,
about Mumma's betraying heart,
in leftover onions.
I look for answers,
will she be okay?
in our neighbors' faces.
Even I don't know
what occupies my heart;
how can I expect
anybody else to show me the way?

I keep my mouth filled
with water,
so no hopeless words birth.

I don't see myself clearly,
I know.
Becoming smaller, and silent,
I pack my bags for India.

JFK: Terminal 4 Airport Lounge

I call up New Delhi;
*the doctors don't know
if you'll make it.*

I pick up my ticket and passport,
and look at the sky ready to bleed.
I pray the rain will hold off
until I reach you.

At first I try to hide the fact,
but any passerby could look inside me
and tell it was fake calm that I was drinking
at the airport lounge in a wine glass.
But, inside that one glass,
I could become invisible.
Inside one sip of wine,
I could whisper my fears.

I play tag with your memories
*I wonder if I am different from you—
I worry how I will preserve
the scent of your memories.*

Ticket and passport in hand
I am ready to leave, praying.
Stepping inside the airplane
not knowing everything will change after today,
I buckle my seat belt.
Not knowing my heart will change
after you leave.

Wait for Me

*I walk inside your heart
my empty palms suture
the leaks in your valves
so you don't drown.*

*I read you passages from our unwritten lives,
convince you to fight harder*

so I don't grieve
for you already.

The flight is set for takeoff
don't ask me to keep the faith

because the sky looks empty.

Looking for Signs

I look at the clouds outside my airplane window;
they don't say much.
The rain beating
tells me a story
about the loss that I am not willing to hear.

What is loss, I ask,
my eyes
pleading for respite.
I am a poet, a writer; how can I not know words?

I forget that I am a daughter, made of flesh and bones,
not just a storyteller sharing metaphors
of what others have lost.

Fifty Minutes from New Delhi

In 2010, I wrote
a poem about strawberries
and how its seeds, like loss, are present everywhere.

On my plane ride to New Delhi,
I think about this fruit, not mangoes,
even though it is summer.
Why, I ask?

I notice the strawberry jam
on my breakfast tray the stewardess brings.
Fifty minutes from New Delhi,
fifty minutes from the secret
doctors would have by now revealed.

Picking up the croissant,
I smear butter and jam on it.
I bite hard, fight to hold the taste;
my teeth ask for mercy.
But I don't stop.
I can't stop.
This is my mom's favorite travel breakfast.
If I can't fight for her life,
I am going to fight for her memory.

Serendipity

My poems are obsessed
with stories of loss and displacement

I tell my husband
as our plane flies over Africa.

Fifteen years, Mummy-Papa lived here, in Libya.
I point out the sun-filled window,
hoping to locate my childhood doors and windows.

Before he responds
the plane turns dark.
Little do I know, the sun has already set in New Delhi
where my mother is playing
Russian Roulette
with death.

Indira Gandhi International Airport: New Delhi

I wait for the yellow roses hiding your face. I stretch out my neck like a giraffe, hoping to get a glimpse of your walking stick. The familiar hug wrapped in your neatly arranged sari. The patches of talcum powder in the curves of your neck. For you to say *Khush raho*, and discuss the lunch and dinner menu. For me to say, *Chilli chicken & noodles, Mumma, can I eat three lunches today?*

I wait. I weep. I sit in the chair in the arrival lounge, holding leftovers of flight food and your memories. People move like dervishes, shadows come and go, reality pours in like black tar.

I am waiting for you at the wrong gate.

FIRE

At the end of the sixteen-hour flight, when we landed in India, Mumma was gone. As Hindu tradition required cremation, I witnessed fire and ashes. I also witnessed the fiery hypocrisy of a few mourners. I fronted a brave face during the day despite the fire in my heart but at night I would break down and pour my heart out in poems.

May 31, 2014

Poetry, pain, and prayers

Bhaiya: "I am sorry. Mom is gone."

Mom was only in her sixties.
How could she abandon Papa, Bhaiya, and me?

How can you do this to us?
How could you not wait for me, Mummy?

New Delhi became a stranger to me;
change was everywhere:
India had a new Prime Minister,
and we had a different structure in our family.

Motherless: I embraced poetry and Bhaiya.
Peaceful and beautiful: Mumma looked
like a poem wrapped in a lavender sheet.

Poetry never once leaves my hand;
pain and prayers never once leave my pen.

Ironically, Mom always complained
that I never wrote poems about her.

Why Didn't You Wait for Me?

Such un-clarity on such a bright day,
such darkness in my verses.

I ask for a sign;
something, anything.

Can you hear me?

Did you know I needed
to give you a hug,
cook some Persian *Kalam Pulao*
when I saw you next?

A detour in your journey,
did you know fate?
Before leaving for Kashmir
did you gather
memories for me?

Why didn't you wait for me?
I ask the same question, over and over again, Ma.

I ask for a sign;
something, anything.
Can you hear me?

I wonder, as I stare at your body wrapped
in blue in the morgue. You look peaceful.
But I want to hear your hot, teasing words:

Chota kapdaa pehnee phir se?

I ask for a sign;
something, anything.
I weep silently,

thanking the thunder
for expressing my pain through the noise.

Why didn't you wait for me, Ma?

Crashing

I can't be a Zen wave in the ocean—
crashing into the shore,
pretending
you never returning is okay.

It's Not Easy

Nothing remains
after Bhaiya and I burn
your body
as per Hindu traditions.

The mourners around us dissolve
into tears;
Bhaiya and I look at each other,
like orphans
lost on the streets of New Delhi,
wondering about our place in the world.

Ghee is what we put into your mouth
and see the teeth marks of death.
Ghee is what you'd add
in our bowl of dal when we were kids.
This history is not easy for us.

It's in our silence
that you hear goodbye.
It's in our tears
that you see the marks your absence left behind.

Noise

I didn't know silence, Ma,
when you were alive.
I will not know silence
in your death.

Conversations with Mumma

I have never learned to sit quietly through confusion. Getting unsolicited, cruel advice from a few people, and putting your body into the fire reminded me why you would say: *You can handle anything, Beta. You are my strong daughter.*

(1)

I was raised to say only words that were nice.
I challenged your behavior, Ma—
wondered why you kept so many secrets,
about those who hurt you.

Why did you accept spiteful words
from those you held close to your heart?

I want to bleed my pain into this poem,
reveal names, expose instances,
but I was raised to say only words
that were nice.

(2)

I know which women showed up to your funeral
to collect gossip. I can smell drama queens
just as effortlessly as I can bathe
in the aroma of your mustard fish curry.

People asked if I took pictures right before we cremated you.
I looked at them in shock.
My mother's dead body will not become an item of entertainment.

I will always be your gatekeeper.

(3)

A hug has never felt so wrong,
I tell you, Ma.
So many people forced themselves
into your living room,
suffocated me with meaningless words.
As their arms held my shoulders tight,
their gaze fixed on the Swarovski crystal on the display mantel.
They kissed my cheek, wiped their tears with the corner of their sari.
A few times they whispered in tones of uncertainty,
your mummy is gone, but think of me as your mother,
even before I had the chance to drink
a glass of water or my sorrows.

I didn't cry or open the chambers to my heart.
My strength intimidated them.

My mother might be gone, but my Papa is not alone.
No one takes my mother's place.

(4)

While your body burned at the crematorium,
my heart turned to ashes at home where vultures hovered
feasting on free food, packing to-go boxes filled with *mithai*.
No emotions, no pain, no guilt.

You fed these scavengers even when you were alive.
You took care of their needs,
even though you saw glimpses of their greed.
Even in your death, they didn't lose the chance to exploit you.

I brought my palm to their faces, hard, in my fantasy.
Fuck off, I wanted to scream:
This is my mother's house, not a shelter for home wreckers.

But I didn't say a thing. I was raised
to say only words that were nice.

(5)

You made mistakes, Mumma;
don't expect me to sugarcoat the truth.
I told you to keep your distance,
but you were so accommodating,
trying to please cold hearts.
Allowing emotional vampires and leeches
into your personal life was a really bad idea.

Was it your heart that betrayed you;
or was it the people you sheltered
who broke your heart?

SARIS and a SINGLE MALT

For Mummy—wherever you are, I bet the place has good whisky and a beautiful collection of saris.

Ode to Mumma

No matter which of your many saris you were wearing
it would set your face aglow—
cotton ones, starched and neatly folded
carrying the scent of sweet cardamom.
Silk saris on hangers pressed
with party and puja conversations;

French chiffons, closest to your heart and the safe in your wardrobe,
never abandoned you on the evenings you welcomed a single malt.

I remember hiding underneath your pallu
when thunderstorms scared me, Ma.
I remember holding the corners of your sari,
twirling until I felt giddy.
I remember the knots in your saris—
your very own mnemonic device.
Beta, these remind me that I need to remember something,
you would say
and then forget what it was you needed to remember.

Memories and scents, I hold them close.
I touch your sari one last time
before we cremate you in your French chiffon.
It smells of cloves and single malt.
I rub it like a magic lamp,
hoping you'd sit up.
Hoping you'd hide me
under your *pallu* one last time.

GRIEF

Everyone has an answer—how to cope and grieve when you have regrets and guilt. But no one tells you how to deal with loss when there is nothing you want to change about your past or your relationship with the deceased.

June 1, 2014

Poetry, pain, and prayers

On Sunday morning, June 1 Mom was cremated.
In traditional Hindu families,
the son performs all the rituals
and women aren't allowed to attend the cremation.

Everybody is clad in white.
People turn vegetarian and give up alcohol— temporarily.
Most don't question anything.

All the traditions and rituals seemed meaningless to me.

Will following these rules bring Mummy back?
Give me the chance to say a last goodbye?
Hug her tight and give her a kiss on her cheek?

Mumma went away suddenly;
I never understood why.
Poetry never once leaves my hand;
pain and prayers never once leave my pen.

Does Grief Wear a Color?

Hindu tradition tells me
to wear white to show loss.

But, will wearing white bring back my mother?

No one answers.

A part of me died with you, Mumma.
A part of me ceased to exist.

I can't wear white,
my bleeding heart will ruin it.

I Write

I write your name
on my lips
over and over again
>   *Mother*
>   *Mom*
>   *Mumma*
>   *Ma.*

This grief isn't supposed to be mine.
This story doesn't belong to me.

I scrub the house clean,
scrape the insides of many bowls,
make chutney out of mint and cilantro,
run a load of dirty laundry;

but nothing washes away
images of you tied
to tubes in the hospital.

I press my palms to my lips:
>   *I don't want to own this poem.*
>   *I don't want to write this poem.*

But loss has a mind of its own.

To survive, I must write.

Forever Courage, Beta

I wear the butterfly pendant you gave me, Mumma. I pull at it, hoping the wings will set me free. I want to get away from everybody. I want to know how to reach you. I don't want to live in the absence of your voice. I wonder what you would say if I read my plea. Suddenly, I hear you whisper in the summer breeze. *Never lose courage, Beta. You've always been strong.* I swallow my angst. Words, I tell you, they stay with me forever.

Namaste

We sit in a car with red lights.
We have brought you home, Ma.
We are in Patna—I can hear the Ganges call out
in a familiar tongue.
There are cops in uniform,
an entourage saying *Namaste* to us,
just the way you would have liked.
Surprise us.
Show up,
give a wave of approval,
remind us the importance of *Namaste*, Mummy.
Take a seat next to the urn—
the pot in which we hold your ashes and your wishes,
of sitting in a government car with red lights and bodyguards,
sacred.

Time Changes Us

I hear you hum, "Time changes us all."
You always complained that I didn't write about you, Ma.
In thirty-six hours, I bled
a book of poems about you.

Writing is what helps me
keep you alive.
Writing is what tells me
don't lose faith.

I stand inside the sound of my words,
like a stranger lost in a dark forest.
I hear you hum, "Time changes us all."

The Final Note

Ma, I didn't permit myself to shed a tear when I found out that you couldn't wait for me. My eyes remained dry when I saw you in the morgue after a fifteen-hour flight. You looked so peaceful; there was unrest in my heart. Next morning, I didn't blink while dressing you up as a bride, applying lipstick to your cold lips with my bare hands, worrying about hurting your beautiful eyes while lining them with *kajal*. I begged the Universe to trade my beating heart for yours. Silently, I helped Bhaiya and others lift up your body and carry it on our shoulders. I stared directly at you as we put ghee and honey in your mouth; *Agni* engulfed your body. *Take care of my mom*, I whispered. In a few minutes, you were gone. We collected your ashes and bones, and put them together with your memories in an urn; I put a lid on my emotions. I emptied your suitcase—the one filled with beautiful clothes for your upcoming vacation. I wondered if you knew you would never see home or *headed for heaven* wasn't just a play on words by the Universe. My heart felt knotted up, like yours. At night I cried while writing poetry, but I didn't cry in front of others. But, on our way back to New York, when the immigration officer asked, *Reason for your India visit?* I said, *my mother passed away*. He put a sticker on my passport; I didn't need to complete an immigration form. I telephoned Bhaiya, *We've been labeled*. I boarded the plane for New York, leaving the international airport in New Delhi, bathed in my tears.

Afterword

When Mom passed away suddenly, it changed my reality. It wasn't just losing her so unexpectedly that made me pause; it was also my reaction to her death that shook me.

Missing her was one thing, but this was different. I wasn't depressed, but I felt no peace within. *Why was I so unhappy?*

Recognizing Obstacles

In August 2014, three months after my mom died, I honored *Ganesh Chaturthi*. It's a Hindu holiday that my mother always celebrated. In yoga class that day, and the following weeks, we talked about recognizing and removing obstacles in our lives, known as *kleshas* in Sanskrit.

One day, after meditation, I realized *I have become an obstacle in the way of my own happiness*. Since then, I have recognized five ways for me to be happy again.

Be true to myself

With Mom gone, I voluntarily took up the role of the matriarch and relationship maintainer, even though there was no real reason or need for me to do so.

While I do believe in maintaining relationships and being kind to all, I also believe that respect has to be earned, and that not everyone deserves our energy. My mom, on the other hand, was okay with nurturing one-sided relationships.

When I tried to manage my personal life like my mother, I started to feel like an impostor. No wonder, in this newly acquired role, I had started to become cynical, which was not who I was at all. I needed to respect my individuality.

Be honest in my expectations

I had expectations (nothing materialistic) of friends and family, and even of the vicious women my mom had nurtured, to at least show up emotionally, as I had for them when they lost a parent, or a child, or a sibling, or even a job. When they didn't, it hurt.

However, it was unfair of me to expect anyone to understand my journey if they hadn't traveled a similar path.

Just because I'd suffered a life-altering loss, not everyone else's life had changed.

Be responsible

Life is like an airplane with low cabin pressure. *When the oxygen level goes down, place the mask on yourself first before sharing it with others, if necessary.* I did the opposite. I paid no attention to my own needs and continued to live by the societal rulebook for "good and cultured women" who place the needs of others before their own. I ignored my grieving by helping others, instead of taking care of my needs.

Be protective of my time

I spent too much time in support of others' needs—listening to them, helping them, and not paying attention to myself. I needed to set boundaries.

Be grateful

In my post-Mom world, even if unintentionally, I focused on those who hurt me by not being there when I needed them. But I took for granted the positive people in my life—the ones who stood by me during my days of grieving and helped me heal. I had focused my energy on negativity instead of expressing gratitude to friends and family who made sure I didn't feel alone in a motherless world.

It's been two years since my mother's death. It hasn't been easy. But, through flight, fire, and grief—and the writing of poems, I've taken a look back and a look inward, and today I feel at peace.

About the Author

Sweta Srivastava Vikram, featured by Asian Fusion as "one of the most influential Asians of our time," is an award-winning writer, five-time Pushcart Prize nominee, Amazon bestselling author of ten books, novelist, poet, essayist, columnist, and wellness practitioner who currently lives in New York City with her husband. Her work has appeared in several anthologies, literary journals, and online publications across nine countries on three continents. A graduate of Columbia University, Sweta performs her work, teaches creative writing workshops, and gives talks at universities and schools across the globe.

Visit the author's website at www.swetavikram.com

Also by Sweta Srivastava Vikram

Poetry
Because All is Not Lost
Kaleidoscope: An Asian Journey of Colors
Whispering Woes of Ganges & Zambezi
Not All Birds Sing
Beyond the Scent of Sorrow
No Ocean Here
Wet Silence

Fiction
Perfectly Untraditional

Nonfiction
Mouth full: *A collection of personal essays and poetry*

Brave New Collection
Honors Women's Spirit Worldwide

No Ocean Here bears moving accounts of women and girls in certain developing and underdeveloped countries. The book raises concern, and chronicles the socio-cultural conditions of women in parts of Asia, Africa, and the Middle East. The stories, either based on personal interviews or inspired by true stories, are factual, visceral, haunting, and bold narratives, presented in the form of poems.

"Sweta Srivastava Vikram is no ordinary poet. The 44 poems in this slim volume carry the weight of unspeakable horrors and injustices against women. Sweta's words span the globe. Her spare and evocative phrases weave a dark tapestry of oppressive conventions that in the telling and in our reading and hearing, she helps to unravel."

—Kay Chernush, Founder/Director, ArtWorks for Freedom

ISBN 978-1-61599-157-0
From Modern History Press
www.ModernHistoryPress.com

Beyond the Scent of Sorrow **delves into the challenges faced by women on a global level**

The eucalyptus trees in southwest Portugal are used as an archetype to symbolically elicit the challenges women face in today's world. Boldly, the poems which are lyrical, literal, short, and succinct, profess the unkind capabilities of mankind.

"Sweta's poetic voice flows like water smoothing and shaping stones. With great skill she uncovers, sometimes tenderly and other times more forcefully, the shroud of fog surrounding the feminine archetype... she has created and nurtured a garden, a wordscape, in which trust and healing can flourish."
—Nick Purdon, author of *The Road-shaped Heart*

"Sweta Srivastava Vikram holds her work close. Fold it one way, a poem of loss appears. Fold it yet again for a poem of longing. Her work is as structurally sound as the elements. It soars with anticipation. Vikram reveals lovely and powerful poems that will long linger."
—Doug Mathewson, Editor *Blink-Ink*

ISBN 978-1-61599-097-9
From Modern History Press
www.ModernHistoryPress.com

www.ingramcontent.com/pod-product-compliance
Lightning Source LLC
Chambersburg PA
CBHW061306040426
42444CB00010B/2548